Real Estate Revealed

Insider secrets to educate yourself when buying and selling, and how to protect yourself from being ripped off in an industry that lacks transparency

Tim Hong

This book is NOT intended to slander any Agent. It is NOT intended to solicit any property already listed for sale. The opinions expressed in this report are those of the author, not necessarily those of the broker or any other party and is protected under Section 2 of the Canadian Charter of Rights and Freedoms - Freedom of Speech. This book is designed to provide accurate and authoritative information in regard to the subject matter. While every effort has been made to ensure factual accuracy, no warranties concerning such acts are made. This book is published for general information and entertainment purposes only. It is made available with the understanding that the author is not engaged in rendering legal advice in any manner or capacity whatsoever. If legal advice or other expert assistance is required, the services of a competent professional person should be sought.
No part of this book may be reproduced, stores in a retrieval system or transmitted by any means without the written permission of the author.

CONTENTS

ACKNOWLEDGMENTS

I'd first like to thank my wife Kirsten, my son Jayden, and my dog, Chance for supporting me through this journey. Jayden is almost 3, and he doesn't know this, but he's the reason and motivation for what I do.

I want to thank my parents who have instilled good values in me, and have given me guidance and words of wisdom throughout the years to help me pursue the personal and career path that I have chosen.

I'd also like to thank Tom and Nick Karadza of Rock Star Inner Circle for kick-starting my investing and professional career and the team members of Rock Star Real Estate for allowing me to surround myself with true professionals.

Lastly, I want to give a shout-out to all my family and friends that have allowed me to bounce my crazy ideas off of, and provided feedback and support throughout this journey.

1. INTRODUCTION

The creation of this book has been a long time in the making. Something I wanted to do for awhile, but never had the chance to put all my thoughts together. Now that I have, I can share my experiences and my stories so that you, as a Buyer or Seller can be confident about the decisions you make. I'll get into that later, but first, let me tell you my story.

When I first got involved in real estate back in 2005, I was working a full-time job in the market research and marketing field and I was fortunate enough for my parents to put a down payment for a downtown Toronto condo. I was living in the master bedroom of a 2 bedroom + den condo, and I was renting out the other bedroom and the den to University students to supplement my rent payments to my parents to cover their mortgage.

Over the next couple years, I started reading more and more about real estate investing. I attended some seminars from Donald Trump and Rich Dad Poor Dad, but they were all US based. After some searching, I finally stumbled upon a local investment group called the Rock Star Inner Circle. With their help and coaching, the first home I actually purchased wasn't even for myself, it was an investment property in Kitchener. I continued to study real estate investing, participating in classes, attending events and learning a lot along the way while picking up a couple more single family homes and a 6 unit building.

The direction towards real estate was something I could see myself going into. I decided to get my real estate license to get access to more information. It was a part-time gig at first helping some family and friends, but shortly after being licensed, I actually ended up getting laid off from my marketing job in the Spring of 2012.

On the drive home after getting laid off, I felt my stomach drop and called my parents. I was kind of scared and excited at the same time. After a good chat with my parents, I realized that this was actually a blessing in disguise as it allowed me to pursue my passion of real estate full-time and I decided to join Rock Star Real Estate.

I started by focusing on helping investors with different real estate strategies, crunching numbers, finding good cash flowing properties and protecting them from bad investments.

Since joining Rock Star, the team has helped hundreds of investors to purchase good properties in good neighbourhoods that attract quality tenants and build millions worth of equity.

In December of 2012, my son Jayden was born and I decided I needed a bit of a change. At that time, I was driving quite often between Kitchener, Hamilton, Barrie and Oshawa to find these investment properties, and I wanted to spend some more time closer to home in Mississauga. So, I started to focus on the "other side" of the industry, helping Buyers and Sellers with their personal homes.

It might have been because I was dealing a lot with investors to start, but for some reason, I noticed more and more that the ethical conduct I was providing to the investors seemed to be lacking with the real estate Agents who were dealing with Buyers and Sellers and their personal home.

What I realized was that the real estate industry in general was missing transparent information...all the messaging I was seeing within the industry was ego-driven, sales-pitch type advertisements that talked about free market evaluations, need more listings signs, your home sold in 30 days "guarantees", fridge magnets and recipe cards.

But there wasn't enough information.

So that's what got me thinking. How do I apply the principles of education and protection to Buyers and Sellers with their personal homes, similar to what I was doing with investors and their investment properties.

The number one reasons from all the stories I have heard from people who were hesitant to get involved with a real estate was **lack of trust.**

Probably to some degree, everyone has fallen into this category. And through my years, I've seen so many people get ripped off, lied to and mislead.

You might have seen or heard of this statistic before, but there's about an 80% turnover rate for real estate Agents within 3 to 5 years. That's ALOT. It's also stated that about 71% of Agents sell less than 6 homes per year.

Truthfully, to become a real estate Agent is quite simple. As I'm writing this book, it only takes 3 courses plus 3 exams to be considered "licensed to sell".

But with the stats so stacked against Agents when they first get into the business, a lot of them will do anything to get that next deal...**even if it's at the expense of the Buyer and Seller.**

Now let me be crystal clear, not all Agents are like this. There are some very good ones out there, but I've seen enough in this industry that I want to bring you behind the scenes, to be transparent with you, educate you, and protect you.

A lot of people within the real estate industry might be mad at me for disclosing a lot of this information – but I feel this is something you, as the Buyer or Seller should know.

There's 4 different sections that lay it all out. The first part is giving you a behind the scenes look at what a "typical Agent" does. The following part is about helping Buyers and protecting them through the process so they don't overpay for a home. The next section reveals the truth about home selling and how to apply investment strategies to create value so you can put the most money in your pocket. The last section uncovers the unethical lies and scams of the real estate industry

2. THE "TYPICAL" AGENT

To understand the whole picture, you have to have an idea what an Agent goes through so you know why they are doing this.

As a real estate Agent, you've already got a mark on your back once you become licensed. There's numerous reports and polls that state the general public's perception of a real estate Agents is viewed, and ranked as one of the lowest professions similar to used car salesmen, telemarketers and politicians.

Typically, the very first thing a new Agent is trained to do is to call friends, family, past colleagues etc. and let them know they are in the industry - I actually think this is a great way to start, however once you have exhausted this list (or you are in a brand new area and don't know anyone), then door knocking, cold calling and prospecting are the next steps.

This is actually general sales knowledge, but what I also call the "annoyance stage". Social cues show that people generally don't like to be interrupted during dinner, called non-stop about asking to buy or sell or being solicited for business in general, that's why we have the Do Not Call lists.

With this perceived negative reputation that real estate Agents get, the general public will automatically put up a "caution barrier" when speaking to an Agent for the first time.

The typical sales script an Agent will ask you is this…

1) Where are you looking to move
2) When are you looking to move
3) Are you a first time Buyer or are you selling a home
4) Are you pre-approved for a mortgage

If you look at the questions, it's all about the Agent trying to qualify you if you're a good "lead". And if you fit the right profile, you'll get a pitch for an appointment.

No where in those questions, is there anything about **providing information** to you as the Buyer or Seller first.

You see, I used to do all of this, and I hated it. It didn't match my core beliefs and how I was raised. Something that I was taught when I was little followed a version of the "Golden Rule - One should treat others as one would like others to treat oneself".

I don't like people interrupting me during dinner, knocking on my door or harassed on the phone every few days about a service or product.

This might resonate with your thinking as well, but when I want something, I like to get information first and then make a decision from there.

The same process should be done before you move. Your first step should be information gathering. This is probably the biggest investment in your life.

Wouldn't it be your in your best interest to know some of the ins and outs before making a decision?

3. PROTECTING BUYERS

Searching for Homes

About 9 in 10 people start their home search online. The largest public site is Realtor.ca (MLS.ca). This is where you should initially start browsing for homes because it pulls directly from the Realtor databases (I'll get into what that is a bit later).

There are also a variety of other sites out there that provide listings, but typically they don't have everything available, and they'll request for more information (name, email, phone) before you can view properties on the site

These websites are called "lead generation" sites. Some of them actually look nicer and are more user-friendly than Realtor.ca, but these websites actually pull a different feed from the Realtor databases, and not all listings are readily available – only about 80% of them.

Other ways Buyer's tend to search for homes include driving around and looking for lawn signs, looking in the classified ads section and attending open houses – but these three methods aren't nearly as effective in getting first access to the newest listings.

What you really want to do when searching for homes is get setup on the Realtor database for email alerts. This is the database that Agents use to upload homes to, so you'll get the most up to date information.

To get access though, a Realtor will have to set you up as it's not available to the general public.

A quick side story to tell you how important getting emails from the Realtor database is. I was helping a newly married couple with their first home. They were already setup on the Realtor Database with me and an alert came up on the Thursday evening. We went to see the home on Friday and put in an offer on Saturday and with a little negotiation, it got accepted. There wasn't even a sign on the lawn and the Sellers cancelled the open house that was going to happen on Sunday. We beat out the general public and they got to move into their new home.

That's why the Realtor Database should be your number one source when you're serious about looking for a home. When home listings are uploaded into the Realtor Database, about 24-48 hours after, the information will be populated to Realtor.ca and the other "lead generation" websites.

If you're not a real estate Agent, you can't login into the Realtor Database, but you should be setup on an email alert that matches the homes that meet your criteria. That way, you'll be getting the most up to date listings out there and won't be missing out on any good deals.

Visiting Homes

So once you see something you like, the common practice (for both Buyer and Agent) is that you will call the name or number that is attached to that home and ask to view it.

The majority of Agents will probably leap at your call and take you to the home, but this isn't actually beneficial for you as a Buyer.

The first thing is that you don't even know who the Agent is, who they represent and if you can even trust them. Think about that for a second, how much trust would you place in someone that you're meeting for the first time and showing you the home to help you purchase something that's worth hundreds of thousands of dollars? Is that Agent representing the Seller or is that Agent just trying to pick up leads?

I believe that an initial consultation meeting is mandatory prior to taking anyone to see homes because it allows me to understand your true wants and needs in finding a home, so that I can customize the searches and provide the right resources for you. The second thing, which is actually the most important, is that you get to know me, as a person, and to see if I'm a good fit to help you.

If we are a good fit, next I'll take you on a tour of homes, or what I call market education. This is going to see homes for the purpose of educating yourself (and me) on what you like and don't like. We'll look at some different varieties, in different price ranges and locations. This is similar to test driving a car and gives you a better idea of what you really want, and helps narrow down your criteria.

On average, after market education, I find that Buyers

will purchase a home after seeing 7-9 homes. That might not seem like a lot, but with a focused effort when seeing homes, you know exactly what you're looking for.

The main concept here is becoming educated. I've heard numerous stories of Buyers rushing into purchasing a home when they're not fully educated while being pressured by their Agent because they just want the commission cheque.

Protecting Your Best Interests

When you're looking for a home, you can have two people to choose from to represent you (if you decide to work with a real estate Agent).

The first one is the listing Agent. This is the Agent that typically has their face on the lawn sign. They actually have the Seller's best interest in mind. How they can help you as a Buyer is that they can show you the home, provide you details about the home and explain the forms and agreements. Remember, they have the Seller's best interest in mind to get them top dollar for their home.

On the flip side, a Buyer's Agent or representative has your best interest in mind when purchasing. Whatever you disclose to them is kept confidential.

Say for example the home you were looking for was $400,000 and you were pre-approved for $450,000. You were highly motivated and needed to move within 30 days and you really loved the home. If you disclosed that information to the listing Agent, who tells the Seller, how much negotiation room would you get from the Seller, with them knowing you're very motivated, love the home and pre-approved for the purchase price? Probably not much, right?

See, the Buyer's Agent should be only disclosing the right information at the right time to put you at an advantage when negotiating. It's like playing cards, you don't show your hand all at once, you play certain cards at certain times to create the advantage.

Also, as a Buyer's Agent, they have a legal duty to protect you through the process by using various conditions and clauses. Their job is to find any pertinent information about the home, the sales around the area to give you an estimated market value, so that when you make an offer, you're comfortable and confident with it.

Making an Educated Offer

When you finally find the home that you want, it's time to make an offer.

This is where a lot of the due diligence and background research come in. The goal of this is determine what true market value is and ways to get the upper hand when negotiating.

Also, this is the time to make sure we add conditions to protect your interest when purchasing such as making sure we can get the mortgage approval, hiring a home inspector or reviewing any condo documents.

When you do a home inspection, it's a visual inspection by an inspector. Unfortunately they can't go putting holes in walls and ripping stuff open like you see on TV.

They can only report on what they see visually and will look at items including foundation, the furnace, air conditioner, plumbing and electrical. Now a days, there's better technology like infrared cameras that help the inspector uncover any current issues.

If there are any major things that do come up during the inspection, then it's something to bring back to the negotiation table.

Negotiating the Offer

This is actually my favourite part. It's trying to get a good deal for you. A lot of people think that negotiating is only about the price, but they don't realize that there are other factors including the closing date, and the terms and conditions in the offer itself.

A lot of it has to do with the positioning of the offer when submitting it to the listing Agent.

If you just submit the offer without explaining the reasons behind the price, terms and conditions, typically the price is the only thing that matters.

If you tell a story, a reason why you're submitting the offer, it gives the chance for the Seller to disconnect from the price itself.

I was helping a couple with an offer on a home we found. The list price was $629,000. Once we did our due diligence and research, we pegged market value to be in the low $600's. This was in a Seller's market (i.e. more demand than supply), so how do we justify getting the price lower?

Well, we submitted an offer for $588,000 and built a story around why we're submitting this offer. We also knew the Seller hadn't found a new home to move to once they sold this one, so we gave them a longer closing date that allowed them the flexibility to take their time to find something else.

This got us off to a good start in the negotiations, and we ended up finalizing the price at $600,000.

Without giving a reason behind our offer, I'm 100% certain that the Seller would have considered our offer a "lowball offer" and disregarded it completely.

Another thing with the price, is don't take the "list price" with too much emphasis. If after the research, we find that the market value is higher than the list price, it's worth paying more and you're still getting a good deal.

The situation you want to avoid is that if the market value is less than the list price – you don't want to be purchasing that home because you take on a lot of risk with having the rest of the market and neighbourhood trying to catch up to your price.

During the negotiations, you as the Buyer want to

remove the emotion from the purchase process – even if you love the home. I've seen time and time again that Buyers fall in love with the home and pay over market value for it – I'm not too sure if it's their decision to take the risk or if it was the Agent pressuring them because they wanted that commission cheque, but it's not a the greatest situation to get yourself into.

Recently, I was putting in an offer for a family of 4 and we were in a competitive offer situation (i.e. more than one offer). The home was listed at $489,000 and we pegged market value around $510,000 to $515,000 based on size, condition and recent sales. We ended up putting an offer at $510,000, but we didn't win.

I found out after the winning offer was $540,000 – that's $30,000 more than ours!

There was no data that supported that home was worth that much and it looked like the Buyer got too emotional about it.

The family I was helping out was actually pre-approved for more than what we bid, but I want to make sure I'm doing the right thing and telling you what market value so I can help and guide you as the Buyer to a comfortable and confident decision.

Final Thoughts on Protecting Buyers

Whoever you get to represent you during the purchase process, make sure they act like a co-pilot and help guide you to the right destination (decision).

You should feel no pressure from the Agent, and if at anytime you have a "bad gut feel" about them, ask the Agent to cancel the Buyer representation agreement, if they won't – go to the broker of record at their brokerage and ask directly.

Fast Start Special Gift #1

If you're starting to look for a home, and want the most up to date listings available **directly from Realtor database** setup, fill out what you're looking for here: **www.timhong.ca/listings**

I'll set you up with homes that match your criteria at no cost, and no obligation…once the time is right, we'll have an initial consultation meeting to see if we're a good fit to work together.

If we are – great! We'll go out for a market education tour and I'll guide you step-by-step until you find the right home and I'll protect you by making sure you're not overpaying and negotiating for the best deal.

---

4. CREATING VALUE WHEN SELLING YOUR HOME

Have you wondered why your house must sell for something similar to the neighbours down the street? This is called the traditional "price driven approach" where you see your classic "free home evaluation" from Agents because they base what you can sell your home for on a fixed price based on others in the area.

It's not a bad guideline to start, but have you ever noticed the wealthiest investors care more about value than price itself? Warren Buffet said, "Price is what you pay, value is what you get".

You see, Warren Buffet invests differently from a lot of investors out there. He doesn't really care for the price of the companies, more so the hidden ways to increase the value of the company.

This is what we call the Value Driven Approach.

Just like Buffet does with companies, we find ways to increase the value, better said, the "perceived value" of your home.

These same principles are the ones we have actually used to help investors differentiate their rental properties to attract top of the line tenants and charge above market rent.

How do we do this?

We tap into the emotional triggers of humans (i.e. Buyers). Think back to a time where you really wanted something for your favourite hobby, pet, or kids. The price didn't really matter did it? You saw the value in it and the emotional high of getting it.

I was in the Disney Store with my 2 year old son and he picked up a toy car from the movie Cars and said "da da buy" – I asked him if he really wanted it and he nodded his head and said "please – love you".

I couldn't help myself but buy him that $6 toy even though he had a handful of toy cars at home already.

That's the emotion kicking in, and that's the same type of emotion we want Buyers to feel when they walk into your home. We want Buyers to not just like your home, but to love it.

When Buyers make decisions based on emotion, they are more likely to make a higher offer.

This is done with a **5-Step Strategy.**

Strategy #1:

Understanding Market Absorption Data

Traditional "property comparable data" is not enough. If you can understand what the market is "absorbing" in property sales at this exact moment, not only can you spot trends, you can take advantage of them.

Basic economic theory teaches us about supply and demand. If there's more demand than there is supply, prices go up and vice versa is true.

Here's a list of the fundamental real estate market absorption data that has helps you understand the current state of the real estate market:

* Current Number of Homes on The Market
* Current Days on The Market
* Number of Homes Sold This Year
* Average Number of Days To Sell
* # of Homes That Sold in the Past 12 Months
* # of Homes That Didn't Sell in the Past 12 Months
* Number of Homes Sold This Month

With this data we calculate the inventory and the absorption rate to see exactly what the real estate market is doing in "real time" and use the data to our benefit to sometimes extract 5-10% more compared to the average home.

Strategy #2:

First Impressions Do Count

This might seem simple enough, but surprisingly a lot of Sellers (and Agents) don't get it. About 9 in 10 Buyers start their search online, and if you can't capture their attention there – you have potentially lost that Buyer.

The more Buyers eyes we can get in front of, the greater possibility of getting an offer.

That's why with professional photos you have to tell a story about your home. You have one chance to make that first impression – so do it right.

At any given time, I can login to the Realtor Database and it still amazes me how some Sellers will allow their listing to have one picture and no description, and sometimes even no pictures.

Even if there are pictures, they have the poorest quality photos. This actually upsets me to see this in the industry. I don't understand how Sellers are willing, or if they even realize how their home looks on the market.

When you're selling the largest investment of your life, take some good pictures. And NO, a camera phone doesn't count.

We get the professionals in, it's not just the camera and lighting, also the angles and how the picture can help a Buyer visualize the home.

In addition to photos, using video enhances that visualization for Buyers. And I'm not talking still photos that zoom in and out as a "virtual tour". I'm talking about someone strapping an HD video on themselves and walking through the home like you would be if you're inside.

Photos and videos are just one part of the online marketing aspect. The way we write about the home is also very important. It isn't your typical 3 beds, 2 baths, finished basement feature based writing. We market the lifestyle and benefits of your home - how you've been living in so that a Buyer can imagine themselves living in it too.

Compare "Beautiful detached home, backs onto ravine, 3 bedrooms, master en-suite, walk-out basement, no carpet throughout" to...

"Enjoy a cup of coffee from your kitchen while you look out into your quiet, tranquil ravine backyard. Appreciate your private master en-suite so you don't have to share. The walk-out basement allows easy access when playing sports with the kids and with no carpet inside the house, it makes it very easy to clean."

Lifestyle writing is typically longer because it expands into the benefits of each feature.

Other examples can play on milestones and activities. If you've seen your baby crawl across the laminate floors for the first time, we talk about it. If you had all your friends and family over for Thanksgiving dinner in your large open concept dining room and kitchen that allows you to entertain easily – all these points help the new Buyer envision themselves there too.

I've seen it time and time again, the better the first impression, the more money in your pocket and we've partnered up with the professionals to help you create that first impression.

Strategy #3:

Creating the WOW Factor

When you think of a five star hotel vs. a 3 star hotel what comes to mind? Even if you haven't been in either, you already have an understanding that the 5 star hotel will have spacious lobbies, great customer service, valet parking, staff waiting to help you carry your bags and when you get to the room, the sheets on the bed are crisp and clean, and the bathroom is sparkling with the toilet paper folded in a tiny triangle. Everything is in it's place and it looks good.

On the flip side, when you think of a 3 star hotel, do you have the same expectations or are they already lowered?

We want to create that 5 star hotel feeling and there's two steps to making it happen. The first is cleaning the place like housekeeping would at a 5 star hotel and the second step is strategic staging. That's making your home look like that hotel room.

I know not everyone likes to clean, especially the areas you're not used to cleaning, like window sills, fan covers, the fridge etc. If you can get to all those places, that's great – if not, let's get someone in to do the house cleaning for you. A lot of us, including myself like to "surface clean", meaning that we like the look of clean, but when you get right down to it, it's not that clean. Get in professionals that will get right down to the nitty gritty making sure that your home looks like a 5 star hotel.

Once it's all cleaned, strategic staging is all about dressing the home for sale. Strategies to help de-clutter, choose paint colours, and which repairs and replacements to make.

Even the little things count – change out non-matching door knobs, clover plates, light bulbs – all of these minor things allow the home to show better.

If you were going to the most important job interview of your life, would you rather have a 2 year old pick out your clothes, or would you have a professional stylist pick out your clothes? Which one is more likely to produce a better first impression?

The more you increase the appeal of the home that triggers the Buyer's emotional senses, the more likely they will put an offer. Whether it's a rental or a home for sale, when a house is clean, staged and ready to go on the market, it will rent or sell much faster than if it wasn't.

At the end of the day, the better the house looks inside, the more likely it well have a higher sale price and spend less time on the market, and I'm partnered with the professionals that will help you create that WOW factor.

Strategy #4:

Eliminate Objections

This strategy is all about making sure there's nothing for the Buyer to re-negotiate. If you're in a position of knowledge and facts, you always have the advantage.

Have you ever been in an argument where you didn't have the facts to back you up? It's hard to win the argument right?

Well, when Buyers do a home inspection on your home, there's the chance they can "come up with some issues" and try to re-negotiate the price that was already agreed upon, or try to make you, the Seller do more things to fix the home and or discount the price even more.

What if there was a way to avoid all that?

That's where the pre-inspection comes in. That's getting a home inspection as the Seller.

What this does is allow you to see what a Buyer would be looking for and if something does come up, allows you to fix the problem before putting the home for sale. This way, you'll have already addressed any "issues" that the Buyer could've brought up.

I use inspectors with the latest technology such as infrared cameras that allow to see temperature changes, kind of like "x-ray vision" to determine potential water leaks and electrical issues.

Another way to help eliminate all objections and put you in full control is certified warranties.

What if you could provide the new Buyer a 1 year warranty on all your major appliances such as fridge, stove, dishwasher, washer and dryer and on your heating and cool system like your furnace and air conditioner?

When a Buyer buys a home, once the home closes, any issues are typically on the Buyer. This is what we call "Buyer's Beware".

But what if you could alleviate all of that stress that the Buyer may have with that 1 year warranty on those major items, and if something went wrong within that 1 year warranty, they could get it fixed at no charge.

What could a Buyer complain about then?

I've partnered up with a home inspector and warranty service, so it'll be very difficult for a Buyer to have any objections.

Strategy #5:

Creating a BUZZ Factor

When you create a buzz or a need for something, the more likely the people want it and the more likely it'll trigger their emotional buying signals.

Think about the stories you hear for the auctions, one day sales, or new product launches. The weeks leading up to it, all the stores are promoting the sales, discounts and the deals on all their products…but you can't get it until the doors open that day.

Sometimes people are lining up outside the night before, to get access!

I'm not going say people are going to be lining up outside your home, because that'd be a little creepy, but the concept is the same.

How do we do this?

Once the videos and pictures are taken, we post them online right away, even if the home hasn't been uploaded on the Realtor database yet.

This allows the "internet" to start indexing pages and when the listing becomes live, then it'll be available for searches and views.

We use a "Coming Soon to MLS" sign on your lawn about 1 week before listing it. This allows neighbours who drive the area, or potential other Buyers who have been in the area looking for other homes to notice yours and take down the information.

Any calls or inquiries about the home prior to it being live, we keep a track of it, and the day it goes live, we send a phone call or email blast to them notifying it has been live now and they can come see inside.

This is the "buzz" we create before the home gets on the market, and the more eyeballs, the more showings, with the potential for more offers.

It might seem very logical about these 5 strategies, but you'd be surprised at how many Sellers, and Agents aren't utilizing these strategies which could mean that they are leaving thousands of dollars on the table.

A lot of the time, when other Agents pitch "multiple marketing packages", the Seller will want to "save" money and pick one of the cheaper packages.

What they don't realize is that by picking these cheaper packages, generally the Agent will do less marketing and not have any professionals come in to do the work required to sell the home for more.

Fast Start Special Gift #2

Because I know selling your home is a huge investment for you, I put all 5 of these strategies to work at a reasonable cost.

Strategy #1 – Understand Market Absorption Data
Strategy #2 – First Impressions Do Count
Strategy #3 – Creating that WOW Factor
Strategy #4 – Eliminate Objections
Strategy #5 – Creating a "Buzz" Factor

To start, get your FREE **market absorption report** about YOUR home with a 30 minute, no cost, no obligation 1-on-1 consultation explaining you the data, just fill in your information here:

www.timhong.ca/market

---

5. REVEALING THE INDUSTRY: AVOID BEING MISLEAD, DECEIVED AND SCAMMED

As mentioned, the real estate industry has a negative reputation, so I'm on mission to change the industry, one person at a time. This part of the book will expose the different tactics that are used to mislead you as the Buyer or Seller.

Before we get into it, now let me reiterate this again, not all Agents are like this, there are some very good ones out there, but I want to be transparent with you so that you can educate yourself and protect yourself when buying or selling your home.

The majority of real estate Agents are 100% commission based salespeople…meaning if they don't close deals, they **do not get paid**. That's zero income. And as you know, with a 80% turnover rate in the first 3-5 years, Agents can get very desperate meaning they'll do anything to get that commission cheque.

Not all of these tactics, programs or techniques are bad, but a lot of them border what I would think is "ethical" so I want to educate you to make sure you're not taken advantage of.

A lot of this information is why the real estate industry is perceived as a negative reputation industry, and the only way to avoid any of these threats is to be understand how they work, and hopefully this section brings you some insight.

Guaranteed Sale Program

If you're a Seller, you probably have heard a variation of this. "I'll sell your home in 30 days, or it's free!" or "Sell your home in 21 days, or I'll buy it!" Did you ever notice that there's always an asterix beside that?

The majority of these programs are what I want to call something similar to "bait and switch". First let's define bait and switch: This is the Wikipedia definition "First, customers are "baited" by merchants' advertising products or services at a low price, but when customers visit the store, they discover that the advertised goods are not available, or the customers are pressured by sales people to consider similar, but higher priced items "switching".

This is the same thing with guaranteed sale programs. Once you realize the criteria to qualify for these programs, the majority of times, you won't qualify because the terms are not favourable to you. So what are these Agents doing? They're baiting you with one type of program, a promise, a hope…but they know that there's a slim chance that you will qualify for the program so they'll switch it to something more favourable for them.

In terms of the marketing side of it, it's a great type of unique selling proposition, but in my opinion, it's quite gimmicky.

To give you the behind the scenes look, this is a

context from another Agent explaining the program. I'm not going to disclose names, more so that you, as a Seller just get the idea behind it:

"You have a home to sell. If I don't sell it in 29 days, I'll sell it for free.

They have to be trading up using us to buy a home and it's at least a 2x trade. I'm just completely comfortable with it.

Yeah, everyone doesn't qualify, but I'm OK with that. Not everyone is going to qualify for everything that I do. That's the number one criteria that kind of kicks everyone out.

First is they have to be buying something else. The fact that you have to agree on a listing price with a Seller - if they're not going to give you a price that's based on reality and you know you're not going to get interest in a property, then they don't qualify for the program.

If they're home is worth $200K and they want to price it at $240K because they think the market's on fire, there is no guarantee. And that's pretty reasonable.

At all times during the listing period, the Seller still has to pay the Buyer's broker. They have to have it staged and inspected. There's a certain price range that you should guarantee.

You have to get your full commission. For us that's

7%, but it could be whatever you want. So if you do sell it, you get your full commission. If they don't want to give you your full commission anyway, they don't qualify for the trade.

Upfront marketing fee of $1,495. So worst case, you're getting an upfront marketing fee.

Price reductions. If you're uncomfortable with price reductions, then just make sure you price this home right out of the gate.

Every 7 days we have price reductions - 2% from the current asking price."

Not all guaranteed sale programs are like this, but are very similar.

If you dissect this one example above...

1) The Seller has to be buying something to qualify for the program – This just allows the Agent to make more commission on the buying side of the transaction.

2) The home has to be reasonably priced – I agree with this as it should be priced based on market value and **not below it** to guarantee the sale.

3) The Seller has to pay full commission – I think this is reasonable as long as the home is properly marketed because you're supposedly "guaranteeing" a sale.

4) There's an upfront "marketing fee" – This is sleazy, if the Agent doesn't sell it, they still get paid, so technically it's not free.

5) Price reductions every 7 days – If it's a 2% price reduction on a $500,000 home, that's s about $10K a week until it sells, so if it's 29 days, that's almost $40K off.

They position it this way so that you might go with another offering of theirs, or another marketing package. And with them knowing the majority of Sellers will not qualify (or want to qualify) for this program, they pitch something else – just like a "bait and switch" tactic.

Commission For a Buyer Agent

If you have an Agent representing you in the buying process, make sure they explain how the commissions work. Anything that has do to with commissions or referral fees, should be transparent and disclosed.

For example, the industry norm for commission to a Buyer Agent is 2.5%.

In the Ontario Real Estate Association Buyer Representation Agreement form, it states:

"If, during the currency of this Agreement, the Buyer enters into an agreement to purchase any property of the general description indicated above, the Buyer agrees that the brokerage is entitled to be paid a commission of [fill in the blank] of the sale price of the property.

The Buyer agrees to pay directly to the brokerage any deficiency between this amount and the amount, if any, to be paid to the brokerage by a listing brokerage or by the Seller. The Buyer understands that if the brokerage is not to be paid any commission by a listing brokerage or by the Seller, the Buyer will pay the brokerage the full amount of commission indicated above."

The "fill in the blank" noted above is typically 2.5%, the industry norm for a Buyer Agent commission.

A Buyer's Agent gets paid through the Seller and Listing brokerage. If the Seller / Listing brokerage offered only 2.0%, then based on the agreement above (that's filled with 2.5%), you, as the Buyer would have to cough up 0.5% of the sale price!!

I don't charge Buyer's to work with me. I only ask for a commitment so that I can provide all my services and resources at your disposal and it holds me accountable to make sure I do the best for you (no matter the commission)…but what I also do, is cross off the above section in the Buyer Representation Agreement form and write "Commission % to be determined by Seller / Listing brokerage", so that they'll never be a deficit between the amount listed in the Buyer's agreement and the amount the Seller / Listing brokerage is willing to pay, so the Buyer will never have to pay anything extra for being represented.

This is especially true for private sales where the Seller is representing themselves. They may or may not offer the Buyer Agent a commission and a lot of times, Agents will not show you the house because they know they aren't getting paid the typical full 2.5%.

A great test is to pick a private sale and ask your Agent to show you it. If they don't want to show it to you, ask them what the reason is. Then call the Seller directly and ask to see it to verify the reason.

The Real Use of an Open House

So an Agent wants to do several open houses to help "market" the property. It does help get more exposure, but a lot of Agents don't disclose the real reason they do them.

About 1% of home Buyers actually come from an open house. The Agents know this. That means that out of 100 people that go through the home, about 1 of them are serious and will probably purchase it.

The real reason Agents like to do open houses is that it generates potential "Buyer business". That is, the Agent knows that out of the 100 people that come through, 99 of them could be potential Buyers and they could help them purchase another house instead and get that commission.

Over the years, it astonishes me when I go into an

open house, and before I disclose to the open house Agent that I'm also an Agent, they'll ask if I'm working with a Agent, because if not, then they can try to "help me" with finding another home.

Also, a lot of times I've been in open houses where the lights are turned off, the blinds aren't open, the property isn't staged nicely and the open house Agent is on their cell phone talking to someone else.

You as a homeowner are being kicked out of your home for a few hours and are basically letting the Agent use your home as an office to generate leads.

The listing Agent should be trying to sell your home first to potential Buyers that walk through, not try to prospect them as a potential Buyer leads.

"Loss Leader" Advertisements

This is an advertising tactic used that is a "bait and switch" on the Buyer side. You'll see a home advertised in the newspaper typically that looks like a home in the neighbourhood you think it's in. However, there won't be an address on it and the price will seem very low compared to what others have been listed or selling for.

The reason is that the home isn't in the neighbourhood, it's somewhere else completely. Agents do this to generate Buyer leads. The tactic here is that they'll make you want to call about the home because it looks good in the neighbourhood and the price is really low. Once you call, they'll use a standard script response letting you know that the house is in some other town, and it is one of their "out of town" listings, but if you're interested in finding a good home in your neighbourhood, let's set an appointment.

Test it out – look at your next real estate section classified ad and pick a home that seems really low priced for the area it's in and see where it's located. It's highly likely, but not always, located somewhere else.

"Buying Your Listing"

Everyone loves hearing their home is worth more, but when a Agent outright lies about it to inflate the "value" of it without justification, and to play on the Seller's emotions, it just makes me sick. This is what is called "buying your listing".

If the Agent gets lucky and it does sell for a higher price, they look good…but the majority of time, when it sits on the market, and then they have do a price drop, which is usually the case, it's typically blamed "on the market" or "Buyer feedback".

There was this one time where I met with a Seller, and I was fairly new to the industry. I researched and educated myself and let the Seller know the home market value based on their condition compared to others would be around $580K-590K range.

The Seller was a referral from my in-laws, and they found out after the Agent who got the listing suggested selling it for $649K because it's "lucky" and it matched the "lotto numbers".

Guess what happened? I watched that listing for almost 2 months and it price dropped 3 times, and finally ended up selling for $589K.

You're probably wondering why would a listing Agent inflate the value knowing it will sell for less, even though they get paid a % of what it sells for?

There are 2 main reasons. The first, it might be a miracle of a chance it does sell for that high, and therefore they would get more commission. The second reason, and the more common one is that they get to advertise themselves more and generate business...meaning lawn signs, open houses, and potential Buyers and in the back of their head, they know your house is over-priced anyway, so they'll take advantage of the situation.

These scenarios are probably the most common that I've encountered and hopefully I've opened your eyes to help you understand if any of these are happening to you.

And as I mentioned before, not all Agents use these tactics to mislead...but there's always a few bad apples in the bunch that will, so be careful!

Cancelling Your Realtor Agreement

One last thing about protecting yourself when buying or selling your home. If at anytime you feel pressured or rushed, have a bad gut feeling, or just plain out don't like the Agent you are working with...stop working with them and cancel whatever written agreement you have.

A lot of Agents will not disclose that you can cancel the agreement, which makes it feel like you "have" to work with them...but that's not the case. Whether you're being represented as a Buyer, or as a Seller...you do have the right to cancel.

For anyone I work with, I upfront state that I have a "100% Easy Exit Guarantee". That is, if at anytime you feel I'm not the right person, then you can cancel with me, no questions asked.

This has two functions...it allows you to be the one in control, and it also holds me accountable to make sure I'm doing the best job and protecting you throughout the whole process.

ONE FINAL POINT

I want to make it clear to the readers of this book. I repeat, I am not in anyway attempting to belittle or slander or to suggest every real estate Agent in the real estate industry is guilty of one or more of the tactics exposed.

Most are not. I assume most Agents are good people and are as disgusted by these "acts" as am I.

This book is intended to educate and to make Buyers and Sellers aware of the ways they can be taken advantage of and victimized in a real estate transaction.

Using this knowledge should allow you to select one of the good, honest and ethical Agents that do exist in our community.

If you are currently working with an Agent, one of the good-ones, I'd urge you to be loyal and hold that Agent in high-regard.

If you are not currently working with an Agent, this book is intended to give you some valuable insight and information to ensure you're able to accurately evaluate and select a good Agent if making a real estate transaction is in your immediate future.

6. WHAT TO DO NEXT?

So after reading the book, hopefully it has given you some insight into the industry and help you understand how to protect yourself when buying or selling.

This probably will be one of the biggest transaction in your lifetime, that's why I think education is very important.

Even though I have the title of "sales representative", as one of my mentors said, "have the heart of a teacher and you'll touch more lives this way."

What I can do for you is a no cost, no obligation one-on-one consultation to get a better understanding of your needs, whether that be looking for something to buy or trying to create value and sell your home.

You can contact me in two ways and I'll respond within 24 hours.

1) Email: tim@rockstarbrokerage.com

2) Leave a voice mail: 1-888-325-8838

If you're not interested, simply put this book away until you think of moving or selling. Or if you know a friend or family thinking of moving who could benefit form reading this book, to learn how to protect themselves feel free to pass it along.

7. CLIENT TESTIMONIALS

Here's what other clients have said about Tim...

"I was a first time home and condo buyer and came in knowing almost nothing about the process or what I was looking for. Tim was very helpful and resourceful, and I really appreciate how relatively quick and painless he made the process for me. He was available to answer any of my questions at any time, and pointed me to other resources to handle financing and related matters. He dealt with the seller several time when unexpected issues came up, and I have been very satisfied with my condo for almost a year now!"
- Zhouran Li, Mississauga

"Since I recently moved to my condo, the only thing comes in my mind at moment is my first meeting with Tim. In my first meeting he identified the needs and wants that I was looking for. Without wasting any time he found me the condo which I was looking for. I wish him all the best in life and God bless him and congratulate you having him in your team to help people like us with best regards ."
- Omer and Maryam, Mississauga

"Thank you for all your help. Buying a new home can be very hectic and time consuming but Tim made the experience easy. I'm happy to have chosen Tim in the purchase of my first home. He also was very helpful when it came to making final choices on finishes, I am very happy with how everything turned out. In the short time he was knowledgeable and really helped to make things run smoothly. I really appreciate his willingness to help out wherever needed. It's that kind of flexibility and dedication that I respect and admire, I have no reservations recommending Rock Star Real Estate and Tim as realtor to friends and family.!"
– Amanda Tuma, Toronto

"Tim was highly recommended by a friend of a friend, we weren't too familiar with investment properties before meeting Tim for lunch. Tim gave us confidence to purchase our first house within 2 months. Another house on the way... His non-

pressure approach bundled with a realistic view, makes him the BEST coach."
– *Fadi Dawood, Mississauga*

"It was a great pleasure working with Tim. He was very helpful and patient with us in finding the right place for us. We did not have much time to look for a place but Tim worked with us all the way and made time for us to look at different places in a short span of time. We were able to finally find a place with his timely and professional help. He is great to work with and a pleasure doing business with. He is the apotheosis of what you would want in a real estate agent - honest, full of integrity, responsible, responsive and cool headed. I will consider him to be my first choice in dealing with real estate matters."
- *Bhuiyan and Rumpa, Mississauga*

"Dealing with Tim was a wonderful experience and much happiness of purchasing a home. Our conditions were tough and the difference of requirements between myself and my spouse was just vast and that should make the job of any real agent really hard. Tim showed understanding, flexibility, availability (even in weekends he used to respond to requests). Beside his very comfortable approach, he is very savvy in using today's technologies. That in it self was super amazing because in today's market, if you don't have speed like Tim's speed and intelligence in reaching your potential property, you will be missing most of what you liked. I remember this one time when we saw a property online that we loved so much and wanted by all means to see it. It was a Sunday though, believe it or not after insisting on Tim (mistake) he arrived to show us the property (with his wife and baby child in his car). We felt embarrassed and guilty with such kindness and dedication.
- *Halim and Fatma, Mississauga*

"As a first time real estate investor (and home buyer) it was great to work with someone as knowledgeable as Tim. I met with a few real estate agents before meeting Tim but I did not feel any of them really understood the process of purchasing real estate as an investment, nor did I feel confident that they would be able to help me through, what appeared to be, a daunting process. Tim was able to answer all my questions, and as someone who has gone through the process themselves he could easily relate to my situation. It was an easy decision to work with Tim. I never felt pressured into making an offer on a property that I did not feel comfortable with and Tim offered only honest and sincere opinions along the way.

Couldn't be happier with how this has all turned out and I look forward to working with Tim in the future."
- *Corey Bullock, Toronto*

"Tim has to be one of the most patient and diligent agents there is. My wife and I decided to start looking for our first home. We found Tim through a family member and couldn't be happier with the service he provided. Not only did Tim make the process simple, he helped answer our million questions about what everything meant and set us up with a mortgage broker who found us a good rate. We would definitely use Tim again for our next home."
- *Mike and Sharon, Ajax*

FAST START SPECIAL GIFT #1

Get The Most Up to Date Listings Directly From the Realtor Database

This is the same database that ALL Realtors use to get their information.

You will a daily email of all the homes that match what you're looking for. You'll get the address, the price, all available photos – all the same information a Realtor will get without waiting for it to go onto the general public websites.

It will update you daily with what is new and what has had a price change, and it also includes power of sales, bank sales and estate sales.

No cost and no obligation.

Just fill in your criteria by visiting:

>> WWW.TIMHONG.CA/LISTINGS <<

FAST START SPECIAL GIFT #2

How to Use Rarely Discussed Property Data to Forecast the Market and Price Your Home to Sell For the Most Money With Confidence

This is strategy #1 in the 5 step strategy to create value when selling your home.

Real estate is supply and demand driven, and by determining the market absorption rate we can tell if your home should sell quickly and for more money or if we should expect a longer market and a longer market time.

Get your FREE **market absorption report** including a pricing guide that will tell you how to price your home with the current trends.

No cost and no obligation.

Just fill in your information by visiting:

>> WWW.TIMHONG.CA/MARKET <<

ABOUT THE AUTHOR

Tim Hong entered the real estate industry as an investor and purchased his first investment property at the age of 28. He educated himself and quickly became an authority in real estate investing.

After getting laid off from a corporate marketing job, he became a licensed real estate professional coaching other investors to find good properties in good neighbourhoods.

When he had his son in 2012, he decided to focus more on the residential side of the real estate industry and that's where he realized that it lacked transparent information.

Now, he's on a mission to educate home Buyers and Sellers to make sure they are protected and not ripped off while making the biggest purchase of their life.

www.ingramcontent.com/pod-product-compliance
Lightning Source LLC
Chambersburg PA
CBHW071006180526
45168CB00003B/1303